914.6

D1808484

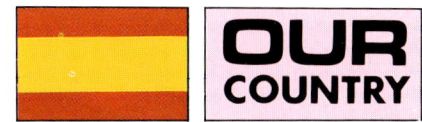

SPAIN

Written and photographed by

David Cumming

PARK MEAD PRIMARY
LIBRARY

SURREY COUNTY LIBRARY

Park Mead C.M. Junior School

GU6 7HB

Wayland

91 636998

Our Country

Australia
Canada
China
France
Greece
India
Italy
Japan
New Zealand
Pakistan
Spain
The Soviet Union
The United Kingdom
The United States
West Germany

Cover *This hilltop village, with its white-painted houses, is typical of many in southwest Spain.*

Editor: Hazel Songhurst
Designer: David Armitage

First published in 1991 by
Wayland (Publishers) Ltd
61 Western Road, Hove
East Sussex BN3 1JD, England

© Copyright 1991 Wayland (Publishers) Ltd

British Library Cataloguing in Publication Data
Cumming, David
  Spain. – (Our country)
  I. Title   II. Series
  914.6

ISBN 1-85210-967-X

Typeset by Dorchester Typesetting Group Ltd
Printed in Italy by Rotolito Lombarda S.p.A.
Bound in France by A.G.M.

All words printed in **bold** are explained in the glossary on page 30.

Contents

We live in Spain 4

The weather 6

Farming and fishing 8

Industry and jobs 10

Schools 12

Religion 14

Holidays and festivals 16

Homes 18

Sports and pastimes 20

Food and drink 22

Shopping 24

Transport 26

Let's discuss Spain 28

Glossary 30

Books to read 31

Index 32

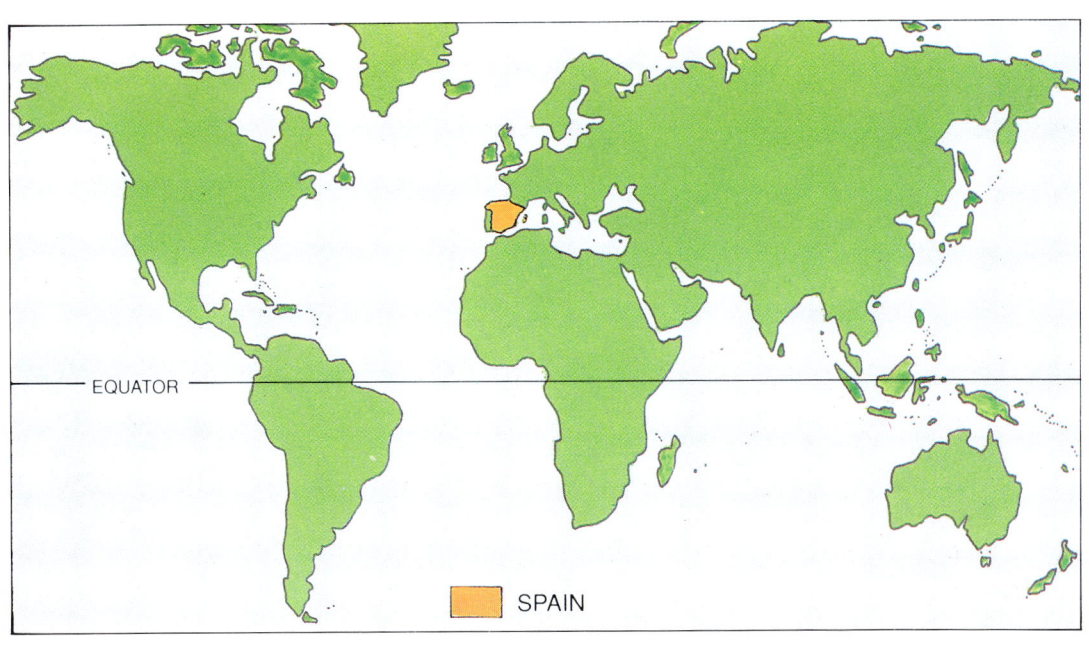

EQUATOR

SPAIN

We live in Spain

This is Puerto de Soller, a seaside town on the island of Majorca.

What do you think of when someone mentions Spain? Sunny weather? Exciting bullfights? Juicy oranges? Spain has all of these, but lots more besides, as you will find out from the twelve children in this book. They are going to tell you all about their lives at home, at school and in Spain's towns and cities.

Spain takes up most of the Iberian **Peninsula**, which is the large piece of land south of France that sticks out into the Atlantic Ocean. The Canary Islands, which include Tenerife, Lanzarote and Gran Canaria in the Atlantic Ocean, and the Balearic Islands – Majorca, Minorca and Ibiza – in the Mediterranean Sea, are also part of Spain.

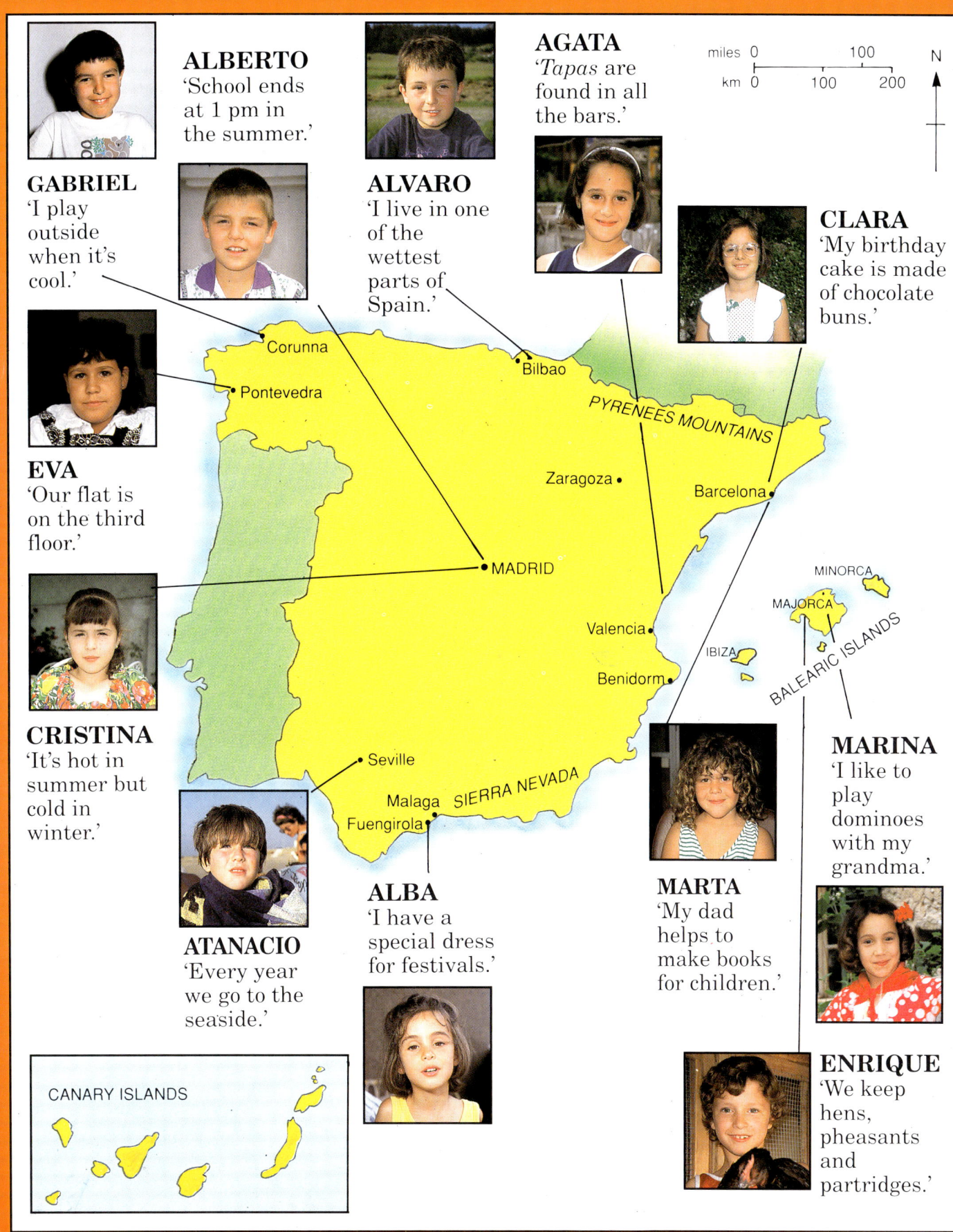

ALBERTO
'School ends at 1 pm in the summer.'

GABRIEL
'I play outside when it's cool.'

ALVARO
'I live in one of the wettest parts of Spain.'

AGATA
'*Tapas* are found in all the bars.'

CLARA
'My birthday cake is made of chocolate buns.'

EVA
'Our flat is on the third floor.'

CRISTINA
'It's hot in summer but cold in winter.'

ATANACIO
'Every year we go to the seaside.'

ALBA
'I have a special dress for festivals.'

MARTA
'My dad helps to make books for children.'

MARINA
'I like to play dominoes with my grandma.'

ENRIQUE
'We keep hens, pheasants and partridges.'

miles 0   100
km 0   100   200

N

Corunna
Pontevedra
Bilbao
PYRENEES MOUNTAINS
Zaragoza
Barcelona
MADRID
Valencia
MINORCA
MAJORCA
IBIZA
BALEARIC ISLANDS
Benidorm
Seville
Malaga   SIERRA NEVADA
Fuengirola

CANARY ISLANDS

The weather

Many people think that Spain is hot and dry all the time, but this is not true. The weather changes during the year and, depending on where in Spain you live, these changes will be big or small.

In the centre of Spain there are big changes in the weather. The summers are very hot and the winters are very cold, and there is little rain. In the south of Spain, the weather is very similar to that in the centre, except that the winters are warmer.

This green valley in the Pyrenees Mountains, on Spain's border with France, will be covered in snow in winter.

'I live in one of the wettest parts of Spain.'

'*Ola*! That's Spanish for 'hallo'. My name is Alvaro. My home is in Guernica, near the north coast. This is one of the wettest parts of Spain and the countryside is very green.'

'In the winter it gets very cold.'

'My name is Cristina. I live in Madrid. It's very hot here in the summer, so I spend a lot of time outside on our patio. Here my grandma is teaching me how to sew. In the winter it gets very cold and we stay indoors.'

The northern parts of Spain have hot summers and cool, rainy winters. In the Balearic Islands and along the coast of the Mediterranean Sea, the summers are hot and dry and the winters are warm, with a little rain.

Out in the Atlantic Ocean, the weather in the Canary Islands hardly changes. Here, it is hot and dry most of the year.

Farming and fishing

Juicy grapes are grown on these vines in the north-east of Spain. They are picked in September and used to make wine.

Farming is still very important in Spain even though many farmers have sold their land and moved to the cities to work in **factories**.

Much of Spain's farming land is used for growing **crops**, especially wheat and barley. Olives and many kinds of fruit are also farmed. The olives can be eaten, or crushed and squeezed to make olive-oil. Much of the fruit, such as oranges, peaches, lemons and melons, is sold to other countries. Grapes, too, are grown all over Spain and many of them are used to make wine.

In the centre of Spain, farmers keep sheep for their wool. In the north, cattle are kept for their milk and meat.

'Our friend catches sardines, hake and tuna fish.'

'I am Agata. I live in Castellon. It has a harbour full of fishing boats. This one belongs to a friend of ours. He sails out into the Mediterranean Sea to catch sardines, hake and tuna. He sells them at the big fish market.'

'We keep hens, pheasants and partridges.'

'I am Enrique. I live on the island of Majorca. My family has two homes. In the week we live in the city of Palma and at the weekend we go to our house in the countryside. Here we keep partridges and pheasants. We also keep hens for their eggs.'

There are many fishing boats in the harbours along Spain's coast. Fishermen catch fish like hake, sardines, tuna and anchovies. These are sold all over Spain, as well as to other countries.

Industry and jobs

Like many other countries in the world, Spain has a mixture of old and new **industries**. Most older industries are in the north, near **mines** that produce coal and iron **ore**. Some of the coal and the iron ore is used to make iron and steel for heavy industry like shipbuilding.

The iron and steel is also sent to new factories to make cars, machines and household goods, many of which are sold to other countries. In the last few years, Spain has been building factories for making parts for computers.

Here are some of the millions of tourists who visit Spain every year. This is the beach at Benidorm. In the background are hotels.

However, one of the most important industries in Spain does not have any factories where things are made. Can you guess which one it is? The answer is tourism. Every year, 42 million **tourists** from all over the world visit Spain. They spend a lot of money in Spanish shops, hotels and restaurants.

'My dad helps to sell books for children.'

'I am Marta. I live in Barcelona. My dad works for a publishing company which makes lots of books for children. His job is to sell them all over the world. Here I am in his office, looking at the pictures in a new book.'

'Dad builds generators like this one.'

'My name is Clara and I live in the village of Alella, near Barcelona. My dad is an engineer. He helps to build machines like this generator, which makes electricity. It will be used in a hospital.'

Schools

In Spain, all children must go to school from the age of six until they are fourteen. Then they can leave and find a job, or continue their studies and take exams for a place in a **university**.

Most children go to schools run by the government, which are free. There are also private schools, where parents have to pay to send their children.

Lessons begin early in the morning and finish late in the afternoon, after a long break for lunch. This lasts from 1 pm to 3 pm, and most children go home.

A teacher and his class at a school just outside Madrid. Like most schools, this one is run by the government.

In June, it is too hot to have classes in the afternoons, so schools shut at lunchtime.

All schools have two short holidays and a long summer one. The holidays at Christmas and Easter last for one week. In the summer, the schools close from the middle of June until the middle of September.

'The smocks keep our clothes clean at school.'

'I am Enrique. I am playing on a slide in the playground of my school in Palma, the capital city of Majorca. We wear these blue and white smocks to keep our clothes clean. I've just had a music lesson and after school I'm going to a gym club.'

'School finishes at 1 pm in the summer.'

'My name is Alberto. I live just outside Madrid. I am the boy in the purple and white shirt. We have lessons on Spanish, maths, science, geography, art and religion. In the summer, school finishes at 1 pm because it's too hot to learn.'

Religion

A procession on St James's Day in Santiago de Compostela. St James is the most important saint in Spain.

Hundreds of years ago, Spain was ruled by the Romans, who wanted everyone to be Christian. The Romans were conquered by the Moors, who came from North Africa. They brought their own religion, called Islam, to Spain.

About six hundred years ago, a Spanish king and queen, Ferdinand and Isabella, sent troops to attack the Moors and force them out of Spain. Soon Ferdinand and Isabella ruled the whole country. They were **Roman Catholic** Christians and they wanted everyone to practise their religion and not Islam.

The kings and queens who ruled after Ferdinand and Isabella were also Roman

'This is my dress for the Virgin Mary's celebrations.'

My name is Alba and I live in Fuengirola. My family is Roman Catholic. This is the dress I wear for the celebrations in honour of the Virgin Mary. Dancers also wear this type of dress and whirl around clicking their **castanets**.'

'I am a Roman Catholic, like most Spaniards.'

'I am Agata and I am a Roman Catholic, like most people in Spain. I don't go to church a lot, but when I do it's usually to say a prayer and then to light a candle, as I'm doing here.'

Catholics, so their religion remained the most important in Spain.

Today, most Spaniards are Roman Catholic, but many people with different religions also live in Spain. So, if you go there, you will see synagogues, where Jews worship, as well as **mosques**, and churches for Christians who are not Roman Catholics.

Holidays and festivals

All the big **festivals** in Spain celebrate a person or an event in the history of the Roman Catholic Church. The most important time is the week before Easter. In Spain this is called *Semana Santa*, which means 'Holy Week'. Shops and offices close and there are noisy parties and colourful **processions** in the streets. Seville is famous for its Holy Week **celebrations** and thousands of people go there to watch the hundreds of processions passing through the streets until late into the night.

This parade in Fuengirola is part of a festival in honour of the Virgin Mary which is held every July.

'Everybody has a holiday on saints' days.'

'I am Antanacio and today I am on holiday with my family because we are celebrating a saint's day. We are at the seaside. I have just had a swim.

'I am celebrating my eighth birthday.'

'I am Clara, in the red paper hat. I am celebrating my birthday in my garden at home. My dress is a present from my grandma. My mum is lighting the candle on my cake, which is made out of chocolate buns piled on top of each other.'

A **saint**'s birthday is also an occasion for a holiday. Every city, town and village has its own special saint. The saint's birthday is celebrated with a *fiesta*, which is the Spanish word for festival. It is a time for parties, fun-fairs, fireworks, circuses and bullfights. The fun lasts far into the night and no one gets much sleep!

Homes

Since it is hot for most of the year in Spain, houses and flats are built to keep cool. The windows have **shutters** to stop the sun getting in and heating up the rooms. Inside, there are **tiles** on the floors, because they help to make the rooms cool. Tiles are also easier to keep clean, because it is very dusty in a hot, dry country. You will find central heating only in the homes where it gets cold in winter, such as in the north of Spain and in the mountains.

Most Spanish houses are painted white. This helps to keep them cool in the hot summers.

In the country, people live in houses which have their own gardens. In the cities, most people live in flats in tall buildings. Nearly every home has a refrigerator and most families own a washing-machine and a television. But only half the homes in Spain have a telephone.

'We have a flat on the third floor.'

'My name is Eva. My home is in Pontevedra, in the north-west of Spain. We live on the third floor of a small block of flats. Here I am reading at the desk in my bedroom. My favourite books are by Enid Blyton.'

'I live in a large block of flats in Corunna, in northern Spain.'

'I am Gabriel. I live in Corunna, on Spain's windy north coast. My home is in a large block of flats. There's a playground in front where my brother, Gonzalo, and I are playing tennis. I'm the one wearing white.'

Sports and pastimes

Spanish children spend a lot of time outdoors, especially in the summer. For most children there is a swimming-pool nearby where they can meet their friends. They also enjoy playing football, and you will see boys and girls kicking balls about like their heroes in the famous teams in Madrid, Barcelona and Bilbao.

Since it is hot in the middle of the day, children play outside in the mornings and evenings. Most children will still be playing with their friends until late at night, as they often don't go to bed until after midnight.

Men have been fighting bulls in Spain for hundreds of years. Some people are now saying that it is cruel and should be stopped.

Most Spanish families spend their summer holidays in Spain. The people who live in central Spain go to the seaside; while those on the coast travel to the mountains.

In winter, people visit the mountains, especially the Pyrenees (on the border with France) and the Sierra Nevada (near Granada in the south), to go skiing.

'I like to play dominoes with my grandma.'

'My name is Marina and I like to play dominoes with my grandma. She is very good and often beats me. She lives in a cosy flat above the shop my father owns in Pollenca, on the island of Majorca.'

'You don't need a licence for these machines!'

'I am called Alvaro. At weekends my family and I often go to a place in the country where there is a racetrack. I ride one of these machines. It has a motorbike engine and goes very fast. It's GREAT!'

Food and drink

This family are eating gazpacho, followed by paella (a rice dish with fish) for their lunch.

Living in a hot country makes you hungry and thirsty, so Spanish children are always stopping for a drink and to nibble a snack.

Breakfast is called *desayuno* in Spanish. This is usually a glass of milk, or hot chocolate, with toast or a bun. Later in the morning, people eat a sandwich or a bun, with a cold drink like *horchata* (a milky drink made from nuts).

Lunch is the main meal of the day and it is eaten late, at 2.00 or 3.00 in the afternoon. The first course may be *gazpacho* (cold tomato soup), followed by fish or meat with vegetables. For dessert, there is fresh fruit, or ice-cream. The grown-ups drink wine or beer with their food, while children have soft drinks.

'*Tapas* are found in all the bars in Spain.'

'I am Agata and I am having a drink with my parents before lunch. I've got a Coke and my mum and dad are drinking beer. We're nibbling crisps, almonds, olives and squid. These snacks are called *tapas* and they are found in all the bars in Spain.'

'*Mortadella* is my favourite food.'

'My name is Clara and I am having a party. My friends and I are eating sandwiches made from long French bread. Inside, they've got *mortadella* (slices of meat with olives in them). They are delicious and are my favourite food at the moment.'

At about 5 pm children have a snack before going out to play. The last meal of the day, called *cena*, is eaten at about 10 pm. This is often a *tortilla* (an omelette with potatoes and onions).

Shopping

In the country, people buy things at the small shops in their villages, and at the outdoor markets where the farmers come to sell their fruit and vegetables. Many country people also grow their own food.

In the cities, people shop in the small local shops and at the large covered markets found in most Spanish cities. Here, stalls sell fruit, vegetables, fish and meat.

Large **hypermarkets** and shopping centres are being built just outside most cities. Many families shop there because parking the car is easy, and they can buy all they will need for one week in one place.

Many people buy their food at indoor markets like this one in Barcelona. Meat, fruit vegetables, and seafood, can also be bought here.

'This little shop sells all sorts of things.'

'I am Eva and here I am with my mum in the little shop underneath the block of flats where we live. The owner is a very nice man and he sells all sorts of things. It saves us going into the centre of the town when we run out of something.'

'My favourite shop is the sweet shop!'

'I am Agata and I love to eat sweets. Here I am in my favourite shop in Castellon – it's the sweet shop, of course. What a selection they have! It's difficult to know what to choose.'

Shops open at 9 am or 10 am and close for three or four hours in the afternoon, when it is too hot for shopping. During this time, people are at home, eating their lunch and resting. The shops open again at 5 pm or 6 pm, when it is cooler. Many shops stay open until quite late.

Transport

This is a fast express train which travels between important towns and cities.

In Spain, only about half the families own a car. In the countryside, people without cars travel about on the buses. Farmers may use a tractor to get them to the nearest town. In the poor parts of Spain, people travel by horse or donkey, or on a cart pulled by a bullock.

In the cities, parking a car is difficult, and people use buses and taxis instead. In Barcelona and Madrid, people can travel on the underground trains.

There are many ways to travel around Spain. If a family has a car, they may use one of the motorways which join up the important cities. People without cars can travel by coach or train.

Flying by plane is the quickest way to travel, but it is also the most expensive. Many people fly to the Balearic Islands, since it is much quicker than taking the **ferries** which sail there.

'Parking is a terrible problem in Madrid.'

'I am Alberto. Here I am playing with my toy cars. I can't wait to be old enough to drive! My parents' car goes really fast on the motorway. When we go into Madrid, though, we catch a bus and then the Metro (underground) because parking the car is such a problem.'

'There are few buses and no trains.'

'I'm Marina and I live near Pollenca on the island of Majorca. We live in the countryside with our six sheep. We need our two cars to buy the animals' food and to get around. There are very few buses and no trains in this part of the island.'

Let's discuss Spain

The next time you go shopping, see how many things you can find that come from Spain. Look at the labels on fresh fruit and vegetables, and on tins and bottles, even on shirts, shoes and handbags. Try to save the labels which tell you where in Spain something was made. Then, with an atlas for help, draw a big map of Spain and put

Facts

Population: 40 million
Capital: Madrid
Language: Spanish
Money: Peseta
Religion: Mainly Roman Catholic

Visitors to Spain spend a lot of money in shops like these. They can buy all sorts of things to take home to remind them of their holidays.

the labels in the right places. Which areas make the most things? Are there any areas where nothing is made?

Spanish children go to bed very late, often after midnight. This is because the evenings and nights are the coolest times of the day, so that is when they go out to play or to visit their relatives and friends. Would you like to go to bed so late? Would you like to live in a country like Spain, where it can be hotter than 39°C (100°F) in the summer?

Spanish families often visit their friends in the evenings because this is the coolest time of day.

Glossary

Castanets Black wooden shells that dancers hold in their hands and click together as they dance.

Celebration Having a party for a special event, such as for a birthday.

Crops Plants grown for food, like wheat or olive trees.

Factories Large buildings where machines are used to make all sorts of goods.

Ferry A ship for carrying people and goods across a river or a sea.

Festival A time for many parties.

Hypermarket A very big supermarket, usually outside a town or city.

Industry The production of goods for sale.

Mine A place where coal, metals, jewels, etc., are dug out of the ground.

Mosque A place of worship for Muslims, who practise the religion of Islam.

Ore Rock with a metal in it: for example, iron ore is a rock that has the metal iron in it.

Peninsula A big piece of land that is almost completely surrounded by water.

Procession A crowd of people walking along together.

Roman Catholic A person who belongs to the Christian religion that has the Pope as its head.

Saint In the Christian religion, an especially good or brave person.

Shutters Wooden covers, like small doors, over windows. These can be opened and closed.

Tiles Square pieces of hard clay, used to cover floors, walls or roofs.

Tourists People who visit a country for a holiday.

University A place where people go to learn after they have left school.

Books to read

Alberto Lives in Spain by Christa Stadtler (Young Library, 1985)

Children of the World: Spain edited by MaryLee Knowlton and Mark J. Sachner (Gareth Stevens Children's Books: 1989)

Countries of the World: Spain by Manuel Alvaredo and David Cumming (Wayland, 1989)

Let's go to Spain by Jonathan Rutland (Franklin Watts, 1980)

Spain is my Country by Cliff and Bernice Moon (Wayland, 1984)

Usborne Handbook of Spain by Heather and John Leigh and Salvador Ortiz-Carboneres (Usborne, 1980)

Acknowledgements

As well as the parents of the children photographed and interviewed, the author would like to thank the following people for their help: Shelley Noronha, Janet de Saulles, Jane Hawkins, and Professor Marcia Pointon in Brighton; Richard and Heather Baker in Reigate; Joan and Alicia Crespi Salas, Martin Aubert and Cindy Walker of The Academy on Majorca; Paddy Green, Fernando Bieco and the staff of the Colegio Publico Gonzalo Fernandez de Cordoba in Madrid; Geraint Williams and Mary Savage of the English Language Centre, Castellon; Miguel Llobera Canaves and Remei Piqueras in Barcelona; Xavier Pomposa in Guernica; Beatrice Navas in Vejer de la Frontera; Maria Nieto and her family in Seville; and Antonio Nunez in Pontevedra.

Index

Atlantic Ocean **4, 7**

Balearic Islands **4, 7, 27**
Barcelona **11, 24, 26**
bedtime **20, 29**
Benidorm **10**
bullfighting **4, 20**
bullock carts **26**

Canary Islands **4, 7**
cars **24, 26, 27**
cattle **8**
churches **15**
coaches **26**
coal **20**
crops **8**

drinks **22–23**

factories **8, 10**
farmers **8, 24, 26**
farming **8–9**
Ferdinand, King **14**
ferries **27**
festivals **16–17**
fish **9, 22**
fishermen **9**
fishing **8–9**
flats **19, 21, 25**

food **22–3, 24, 25**
football **20**

fruit **4, 8, 22, 24, 28**

holidays **13, 16–17, 21**
Holy Week **16**
homes **18–19**
hotels **10, 11**
houses **18, 19**

industry **10–11**
iron **20**
Isabella, Queen **14**
Islam **14**

jobs **11**

Madrid **12, 13, 26, 27, 29**
Majorca **4, 9, 13, 21**
markets **24**
meals **22**
Mediterranean Sea **4, 7, 9**
Metro **26, 27**
mines **10**
mosques **15**
motorways **26**

olive-oil **8**
olives **8, 23**

population **29**
Pyrenees Mountains **6, 21**

religion **14–15, 29**
restaurants **11**
Roman Catholic Church **14, 15, 16**

St James **14**
Santiago de Compostela **14**
schools **12–13**
Seville **16**
sheep **8, 27**
shipbuilding **10**
shops **11, 24–25, 28**
Sierra Nevada **21**
snacks **22, 23**
sport **20–21**
steel **10**
sweets **25**
swimming **20**
synagogues **15**

tapas **23**
tourism **10, 11, 28**
trains **26**
transport **26–7**

university **12**

weather **4, 6–7, 29**
wine **8, 22**
wool **8**

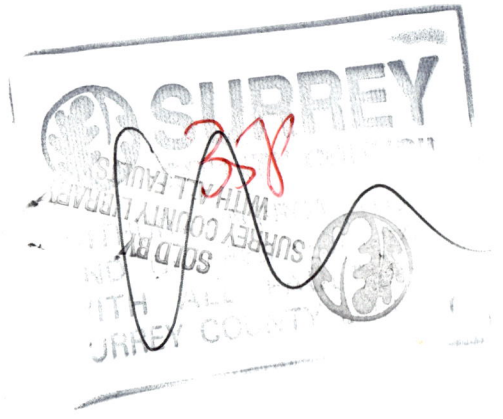